It all started one day in the 1960s.
Bill Moyes, an American water skier,
tied a long kite to the back of a motorboat.
He attached himself to the kite
with a harness.
Then he shouted for the motorboat
to take off.
Moments later, the speeding boat
pulled the kite – and Moyes –
high up into the air.

A motorboat can pull you high into the air.

# HANG GLIDING

## Henry Billings and Melissa Billings

Published in association with The Basic Skills Agency

Hodder & Stoughton

A MEMBER OF THE HODDER HEADLINE GROUP

## Acknowledgements

*Cover: Stone/Getty Images*
*Photos: p. 16 © Allsport; all other photos © Action-Plus Photographic*

Orders: please contact Bookpoint Ltd, 130 Milton Park, Abingdon, Oxon OX14 4SB.
Telephone: (44) 01235 827720, Fax: (44) 01235 400454. Lines are open from 9.00–6.00,
Monday to Saturday, with a 24 hour message answering service.

*British Library Cataloguing in Publication Data*
A catalogue record for this title is available from The British Library

ISBN 0 340 86952 6

Published by Jamestown Publishers,
a division of NTC/Contemporary Publishing Group, Inc.

Copyright © 1996 by NTC/Contemporary Publishing Group, Inc.

First published in UK 1999 by Hodder & Stoughton Educational Publishers.
This edition published 2002
Impression number    10 9 8 7 6 5 4 3 2 1
Year                          2007 2006 2005 2004 2003 2002

Typeset by Fakenham Photosetting Ltd, Fakenham, Norfolk.
Printed in Great Britain for Hodder & Stoughton Educational, a division of Hodder Headline
Plc, 338 Euston Road, London NW1 3BH by The Bath Press Ltd.

It was a great ride.
Moyes looked down at the sparkling water
far below.
He soared through the air,
feeling almost like a bird.

The plan was for the boat driver
to slow the boat down gradually.
That would cause Moyes
to sink slowly back to earth.

But Moyes spotted trouble ahead.
The motorboat was pulling him
towards some high-tension wires.
Moyes did the only thing he could think of.
He undid the rope that tied him to the boat.

Suddenly, Moyes was flying like a bird.
He was no longer connected
to anything on the ground.

A hang glider flies high above the ground.

The wings of the kite kept him from falling.
They caught the wind and allowed him
to glide gently down to earth.
And so he completed the world's first
hang gliding journey.

From then on, Moyes was hooked.
He made lots of flights
with his wings strapped on.
He stopped using a motorboat
to get into the air.
Instead, he just climbed
to the top of a ledge or a cliff
and jumped off.

In 1970, he even soared
over the Grand Canyon.
Others began to follow his lead.
Like Moyes, they used kites
with flexible wings.
They also worked out how to steer
by shifting their weight back and forth.

Hang gliders can float in the sky for hours.

When hang gliding pilots first take off,
they may fall through the air
for three to six metres.
Then their wings catch air currents
and they begin to rise.

By gliding from current to current,
hang gliding pilots can float
among the clouds for hours.
They can make their hang gliders
do loops, dives and turns.
And they can land easily.

These pilots make it look easy.

In some ways it is.

There's no motor to worry about.

There are no controls.

It's just you, your wings and the wind.

It is, as one pilot says

*The closest approach man has to pure flight.*

But hang gliding has a darker side.
It can be dangerous.
In fact, it can be deadly.
More than one pilot has died
while trying to fly a hang glider.
Many others have been badly hurt.

In 1981,
a young man was hang gliding in New Mexico.
For a while, he sailed smoothly
through the air.
Then winds began to carry him
towards some storm clouds.
He found his gentle ride
becoming rougher.

Hang gliding in strong winds can be dangerous.

Soon he found himself
in the middle of a thunderstorm.
He tried to fight his way through it,
but the storm was too strong.
The glider crashed.
The young man did not survive.

In 1993, another young man went hang gliding
in the mountains.
There was very little wind that day.
He decided to add some excitement
to his flight.
He steered his hang glider near some trees,
but he got too close.
He smashed into a tree.
He was so badly injured
that doctors were not sure he would live.
He did live,
but he never fully recovered
from the accident.

It is dangerous to hang glide near trees.

Clearly, thunderstorms and trees
are big dangers.
But there are others as well.

Pilots must be careful not to take off
in winds that are too high.
They have to be especially careful
to avoid rotors.
These are strong winds
that come rolling in off mountains.

Rotors can cut through a normal wind
and send the hang glider
spinning out of control.
They can cause a hang glider
to take a nosedive straight down.
That's called going over the falls.

Sometimes, when pilots go over the falls,
they can steady the hang glider
and bring it safely out of the dive.
But sometimes they can't.
Then, even the best pilots have to bail out.

Safety gear is vital in case you have to bail out.

In the 1993 World Hang Gliding Championships
a top pilot went over the falls.
As he did so,
his body fell against the wings
of his hang glider.
Luckily he was able to open his parachute
and float thousands of metres back to earth.

Pilots also have to look out
for dust devils.
These are tight swirls of air
that lift sand, dirt and bits of litter
off the ground.
They can also lift up a hang glider.

One pilot was caught in a dust devil
in 1993.
His hang glider was pulled up into the air
then smashed back to the ground.
He broke three bones in the crash.

A hang glider has to look out for dust devils.

At times,
pilots seem to be asking for trouble.
They pick takeoff points
that add to the risks.
For instance, some hang gliding pilots
jump off from Dead Horse Point.
That is a 700 metre sandstone cliff
in Utah, America.
At the bottom of the cliff
lie a cactus or two –
and a lot of pointed rocks.
As one man put it

*If you make a mistake going off this cliff,*
*you're dead.*

When another man peered over
Dead Horse Point for the first time,
he felt his stomach turn to knots.
He shouted out

*I can't do it! I can't jump.*

He did jump, but he is not the only one
to have felt that kind of terror.
Many people have struggled
to control their panic
just before takeoff.
As one pilot put it

*It's the fear.*
*It's worse before you launch.*
*Then it's okay.*

A hang glider gets ready to jump.

In fact, once you're in the air,
the ride is much more than simply okay.
It is fantastic.
Pilots say they feel great joy
as they soar high above the earth.
One pilot said

*You're out in the open*
*with nothing around you;*
*sometimes you forget you even have a kite.*

Another said

*You really feel like a bird.*
*You feel the wind on you*
*and the flutter of the sail.*
*It really is like you are a part*
*of the hang glider itself.*

It is that thrill
– the thrill of flying free –
that makes hang gliding so appealing.